The Place Where You Stand

ISBN 978-1-62806-482-7 (print | paperback)
ISBN 978-1-62806-483-4 (ebook)

Library of Congress Control Number 2026907476

Published by Salt Water Media
29 Broad Street, Suite 104
Berlin, MD 21811
www.saltwatermedia.com

Cover art used with license from istockphoto.com
Interior images used with license from istockphoto.com

Author Website: www.lesliepoff.com

The Place Where You Stand

Leslie Poff

Take your sandals off your feet, for the place where you stand is holy ground.

Exodus 3:5, New King James Version

Earth's crammed with heaven,
And every common bush afire with God,
But only he who sees takes off his shoes;
The rest sit round and pluck blackberries.

- Elizabeth Barrett Browning

Contents

INTRODUCTION

I shall be telling this with a sigh
Somewhere ages and ages hence:
Two roads diverged in a wood, and I—
I took the one less traveled by,
And that has made all the difference.

- Robert Frost, "*The Road Not Taken*"

I am a recovering evangelical Christian of the reformed tradition. I no longer hold fast to all the tenets taught to me by that particular religious persuasion, yet I hold much of it dear. I am grateful to the reformed church for launching me on a spiritual journey, but I am also troubled by much of its teachings.

As a teenager, I cut my spiritual teeth in this church. These were some of the best times of my life. I devoured the Bible, viewing it as a love letter written directly to me by the Creator of the universe. I sought and found direction on its pages. Life was simple then, because I knew all the answers. And frankly, I was quite smug and self-righteous—as those who know that they are in the right camp can be.

But here's the thing: In my religious tradition, we did not question what we were taught. To do so would be seen at best as naive, and at worst, heretical. In most traditional religious structures, there is an infallible authority; in the reformed tradition, it is the Bible. The Bible, and the manner in which it has been interpreted by reformed leaders—the vast majority of whom have historically been white heterosexual men—were and are absolute, were and are still to remain unchallenged.

So this was my foundation, my operating system. When you have a strong belief system, it provides security and confidence, and it serves as a filter through which you receive and process information. This works well in an echo chamber. ... turns out that as long as you spend time interacting with people who hold views that dovetail nicely with yours, you can continue feeling secure and confident.

But here's where it gets dicey: Either by happenstance or by choice, if you find yourself bumping up against people who hold views which are different from your own, you might begin to question some of those dearly held tenets. It is said that if you hang around a barbershop long enough, eventually you might find yourself having at least a trim, right?

And getting into that barber chair is, in and of itself, very frightening. Couple that with allowing someone to cut that beautiful hair which you have spent years grooming. The stakes are very high for an evangelical, for whom the questioning of authority and tradition can be seen as stepping out onto a slippery slope. But I have carefully and fearfully embraced other avenues of spirituality over the years, and I am, I believe, a better person for it. I have learned to listen to the God within me, and to find the God in others and in all created things. I no longer labor under the heavy burdens of obligation, either to disapprove of the behavior of others or to defend the honor of God.

I want that freedom for you as well. So I offer these meditations to you—these contemplative musings. I have created a guideline for you to follow, along with suggested activities to assist you in developing a personal contemplative practice. This can serve as a path to a deeper and more joyful experience of God. The outline for this devotional guide is based on the psychological theory that the formation of a habit takes 21 days, but to create a permanent lifestyle change can take up to 90.

This introductory section is provided as you prepare for your journey. Create a plan for success. Carve out a quiet space and time in your day for your new contemplative adventure. Find a nice pen and choose a journal that brings you joy. Light a candle, diffuse some essential oils, play some Enya. I will be holding space for you.

Accept my blessing for you, precious little one, adored by God. I wish for you to be swept up into the wondrous, if sometimes dangerous love of God. I wish for you a road less traveled, and joy on your journey. I wish you shalom. The light in me honors all of the blinding light that you carry within. Namaste.

Journaling is highly recommended as a practice to deepen the experiences suggested in this book. Consider using the weekly questions for reflection as an inspiration for journaling.

Questions for Preparation:

1. What was the reason you chose to read this book?
2. Are there changes you wish to see in your life as a result of working through the book?
3. Define the following terms: contemplation, meditation, mindfulness.
4. How would you describe your faith? Is there a way you would like to deepen it?
5. What does it mean to you to have a contemplative practice?
6. How can you view the next few months of working through this book as an adventure, the pursuit of a road less traveled?

Week 1

Reading: Psalm 4

Stand in awe, and sin not: commune with your own heart upon your bed, and be still.

Psalm 4:4, King James Version

Be still and know that I am God.
I am exalted among the nations and
I am exalted in the earth.

Psalm 46:10, Literal Standard Version

When I was a young and idealistic teenage Christian coming to faith on the coattails of the Jesus movement of the seventies, my faith looked very different than it does now.

Perhaps largely because of church teachings, I approached God in a left-brained manner, feeling mistrustful of any right-brained spirituality. I studied the Bible, theology, and apologetics. I read. I learned. I discussed.

I have become suspicious of this Western approach to faith, as it seems to me that when I seek God with my mind, it is very difficult to separate my own ego, my own desires from the Voice of God. I think that reading and listening can be helpful in learning about spiritual matters, but it is hard (for me, anyway) to read a spiritual text without imposing my own theological filter onto it. I end up in an echo chamber of my own devising—reading, and understanding Scripture which confirms what I already think and believe. I remain unchallenged, my progress stunted.

Have you ever been in a group setting where the leader prayed out loud, and you had the distinct feeling that the prayer was meant to teach you something rather than to lead you to a Divine Encounter?

These are but a few of the pitfalls of left-brained religion, and it seems as if people are running for their lives away from institutions that are founded on thought-based practices. According to the most recent Pew Research Group poll of 36,908 individuals, 49% of Americans age 74 and older state that they attend religious services at least once a month. The numbers decline steadily in the younger age brackets. Only 24% of polled men and women aged 24-34 report attending services.

But spirituality is not dead. There are still pilgrims on the way, seeking encounters with the Divine. You can find them flocking to yoga studios, drumming circles, ecstatic dance gatherings, group meditation, forest bathing, and silent retreats.

Let's pause for a moment.

Be honest: You had a little bit of an attitude toward one or more of the practices listed in the above paragraph, didn't you? It's okay; it's not your fault. You were taught dualistically and came to believe that the spiritual practice with which you are most closely affiliated is the right one—and others are not. But let's suspend our judgment for a moment, shall we?

Maybe, just maybe, if deep calls unto deep (Psalm 42) there are other, and perhaps far more effective means of encountering God than reading a book or listening to a sermon or podcast. When I suspend my thinking as in the contemplative prayer described by Thomas Merton, what if I discover that, as he says:

Unlike other forms of prayer that may involve verbal communication, intercessions, or structured liturgies, contemplative prayer is marked by its intentional embrace of stillness. It is a method of prayer that transcends words and thoughts, aiming instead to meet God in the pure, unspoken depths of the heart.

Perhaps the reason you love camping, or music, or moving your body either athletically or artistically is because you are having a Divine Encounter. Be open to setting aside your crazy-busy, close-minded thinking for a minute and seek God. Upon reflection, you may find yourself murmuring, Indeed the LORD is in this place, and I knew it not.

Questions for Reflection:

1. Do you have a contemplative practice? Are you open to the idea? What will you do to pursue one? If you are already a contemplative, what will you do to deepen your practice?

2. Is it difficult for you in this season to carve out any time for silence? If so, could you perhaps approach your day, your tasks, your obligations, your children in a spirit of mindfulness—being fully present in each moment? Try this just for today. And then, just for today, commit to journaling about the experience.

3. What are your thoughts about spiritual practices that differ from your own? Do you view them as silly ... or dangerous? Is there something you might be willing to try? Maybe the minute of silent meditation suggested this week is enough of a stretch for you. Commit to this practice.

4. What are your thoughts about communicating with God in complete silence? Have you ever tried it? What was your experience?

Contemplative Practice: Our first meditation will last for only two minutes. (You can do this; I promise.) Remember that whenever you meditate, your mind will wander. It likes to think; that's what it is designed to do. Your job is to notice when your mind is wandering and gently disengage from the thought. If it helps, you can picture yourself meditating by a gently flowing river. If a thought pops into your head, simply place it in the river to be carried away.

Find a comfortable place for your meditation. It is usually best to sit upright, but if you can achieve better focus lying down, choose that position. Once you are in your cozy spot, take a deep breath in through your nose, and sigh it out through your mouth. Then, sit quietly, preferably with eyes closed, and begin to engage your other four senses, one by one. Notice what is going on in the world around you. What do you hear? What do you smell? Notice the temperature of the air in the room, or if you are outside, maybe you feel the sun warming your skin. Maybe you feel a gentle breeze.

That is your meditation for this week. You are learning to pay careful attention to the world you inhabit. You are developing mindfulness.

Option: Log in at my website (www.lesliepoff.com) to access guided meditations which accompany this book. Some people find it easier to focus using guided meditation. Others find it distracting. Choose your own adventure.

WEEK 2

READING: MATTHEW 6: 24-33

Consider the lilies of the field, how they grow: they neither toil nor spin; and yet I say to you that even Solomon in all his glory was not arrayed like one of these.

Matthew 6:28-29, New King James Version

The only commandment I ever obeyed -
'Consider the Lilies.'

Emily Dickinson

Some of us are better at growing flowers than others. For those who are not really known for their green thumbs, might I recommend the Tiger Lily?

A neighbor once gave me about twelve of these little babies, and I currently have more than I know what to do with. One gardening website refers to them as tough, long-lived, and tolerant of neglect. The perfect flower.

At first light, they gloriously open their bright orange faces toward the sun, soaking up energy all through the day. When night falls, they yawn and tuck themselves in, gathering their petals in an attitude of surrender.

Did you know there is a Corpse Lily? This huge plant is found in the rainforests of Indonesia and can weigh up to twenty-four pounds. Because it gives off the odor of decaying flesh, it is fondly referred to as the Corpse Flower. Luckily, it is rare.

To be fair, the reading for this week is about more than the mere consideration of lilies; it is about the manner in which the universe seems to be able to unfold without a lot of worry and angst. I like the idea of wandering mindfully through nature and considering the lessons taught by even the smallest and often overlooked created wonders. I like the idea of considering lilies.

There is a wonderful poem written by Mary Oliver called "The Summer Day," describing the spiritual experience of paying attention, of being idle and blessed. The poem dares to suggest that a day spent simply and meditatively, of noticing the mere maneuvering of a grasshopper is a day well spent.

Please take a moment and read this amazing work.

The part of this poem which is most often quoted is its last two lines, along with the challenge to us as to how we will spend the wild and precious life that has been gifted to us.

Maybe it is the last stanza that is most appealing to our

frantic Western mindset, our focus on doing rather than being. How do those last two lines of the poem make you feel? Inadequate? Anxious? If you are anything like me, it makes you want to grab a pen and a calendar and start making lists and goals in order not to waste any more time.

Do yourself a favor and read the whole poem again slowly, allowing the word pictures to form. It brings some questions to mind, doesn't it?

The woman who asks what we will do with our one wild and precious life is the same one who just spent an entire day strolling through a field or two. How much time did she actually spend watching that grasshopper? Idle and blessed? What else should she have done? I imagine that most of us can think of a lot of things that would pile up during a day of grasshopper watching.

But ...

I think one reason this poem is so popular is that deep down, we know she is right: There is breathtaking beauty and mystery in the smallest and simplest of things. We have only to open our senses to them. We have only to consider the lilies, the birds of the air, the grasshoppers.

What if this was the year when we learned how to pay attention? Life is wild and precious, after all.

Questions for Reflection:

1. Have you ever had what you would call a spiritual experience when you were in a natural setting? What did you learn?

2. What does it mean to be idle and blessed? Can you think of a time when you experienced both idleness and a sense of blessing?

3. *There is breathtaking beauty in the smallest and simplest of things.* What is your reaction to this statement?

4. Do yourself a favor and walk or look outside. What can you find within your field of vision that amazes you?

5. The ancient Celts believed there were certain sacred places which they referred to as *thin*. In such places, it seemed that the veil between the natural world and the spiritual realm was especially thin. Have you ever been to such a place? What was your experience there?

6. What do you plan to do with your one wild and precious life?

Contemplative Practice: Are you ready for three minutes of silent meditation? If not, that's okay. Spend as much time in meditation as you can comfortably. Begin as you did last week, by noticing your surroundings with all of your senses. But this time, after you have established a sense of awareness, begin to draw that attention inward and notice your own body. Notice the parts of your body that are touching the ground or your chair. Scan your body and notice any tension you are holding. Do not judge it. Simply bring your loving awareness there and try to relax. If your mind wanders, do not judge that either. Just be aware of it. It is the nature of your mind to think. Just gently bring your awareness back to the loving observation of your body.

Week 3

Reading: Genesis 28: 10-22

"Then Jacob awoke from his sleep and said, 'Surely the LORD is in this place, and I did not know it. How awesome is this place! This is none other than the house of God, and this is the gate of heaven.'"

Genesis 28:16, New King James Version

Very rarely do I remember my dreams, but there have been occasions when I have glimpses of them at some point during the next day. Often something serves as a reminder, and suddenly an element of the dream flashes into my mind.

Time seems to have no meaning in my dreams, and often people who have passed on from this life make an appearance—and this seems perfectly normal. In fact, one night I had a dream in which not one, but two deceased family members were present and spoke words of encouragement. I had this dream a few years ago, yet I remember the highlights to this day.

But here's the thing. The morning after I had that dream, rather than busying myself about my day, I took the time for meditation. As I meditated quietly, the memory of the dream came to me. I was able to reflect on it, mulling it over in my mind. This reflective practice served to gel the memory of the dream, and I am still able to access it.

Do you have a contemplative practice—something that allows you to step back and reflect on your reality? Far too often, we flit from one activity to the next, feeling overwhelmed and stressed. And I do not say this with a critical spirit; the obligations are real, and they are important. And I understand that, short of living in a monastery, reflection often seems elusive—a luxury few of us seem to have.

And yet, and yet ...

Some people seem to be better at prioritizing and recognizing the value of a reflective or contemplative practice. Mahatma Ghandi is quoted as saying *I have so much to do today. I must meditate for two hours instead of one.* Is it possible that taking the time to pray, meditate, or journal could actually make us more productive? Granted, there were no small children clinging to the hem of Ghandi's robe. It can be hard to meditate when there is a fistfight going on in the next room.

Martin Luther King Jr. was 19 years old when Ghandi was assassinated, but King was a student of his principles of nonviolence. He even traveled to India to meet with relatives of Ghandi with the goal of better understanding the idea of seeking truth and love while refusing to participate in something that seemed morally wrong. Like Ghandi, King also recognized the importance of contemplative practices such as prayer, meditation, and reflective writing.

It is hard to minimize the impact of Martin Luther King Jr.'s *Letter from a Birmingham Jail* on the civil rights movement, and one pictures him finally getting some quiet time to collect his thoughts:

King suggests that he is able to write such a long letter only because he is alone in jail, rather than in the comfort of his study and reflects on the fact that for the incarcerated there are fewer distractions, enabling one to think, write and pray extensively. Anne Frank kept a diary during the long hours she was forced to spend locked in a small room, fearful that any noise might result in the demise of her family. Although her diary contained only the private writings of a child, it touched the entire world.

This is my point: If we take the time for reflective practices such as prayer, meditation, or journaling, we can learn to recognize the fingerprints of the Divine in our lives. Often, God is very subtle, coming to us disguised as our reality. If we take the time to pay attention, we may have an *aha* moment just as Jacob did: *Surely the LORD is in this place and I did not know it!* It gets easier with practice.

Questions for Reflection:

1. Have you ever had a dream that deeply impacted you—perhaps one that seemed to contain an important message?
2. Take some time right now to reflect on your past week. What are you grateful for?
3. What has been your past experience with journaling? Are you journaling currently, maybe using the reflection questions in this guide as a starting point?
4. Stop for a moment and consider the effective leadership of Ghandi and subsequently Martin Luther King Jr. What are your thoughts regarding meditation as a means of achieving greater effectiveness?
5. The 14th Dalai Lama advised that meditation is the key to the transformation of the mind. What is your response to this?
6. The apostle Paul taught the Romans: *Do not conform to the pattern of this world, but be transformed by the renewing of your mind. Then you will be able to test and approve what God's will is—his good, pleasing and perfect will.* Compare this to the thoughts of the Dalai Lama mentioned in Question 5.

Contemplative Practice: Last week, we began with a focus on our surroundings, but subsequently drew our attention inward, noticing our own bodies, and bringing breath and relaxation to any place where we held tension. We will begin as we did last week, but this week, after scanning our bodies for tension and breathing relaxation into those areas, we begin to draw attention to our breath. Please do not attempt to change or manipulate it in any way; simply observe it with wonder and gratitude. Notice the parts of your body that move when you breathe. Notice the temperature of your breath as it enters your body, and then as it exits.

This is your meditative practice for the week. In addition, try to remember to pause in the busyness of your day and be amazed and grateful for the ability of your body to draw breath without any conscious effort on your part.

Week 4

Reading: John 20: 19-22

And with that he breathed on them and said,
Receive the Holy Spirit

John 20:22, New King James Version

Qi (chi) is the Chinese term for the energy that runs throughout all of the universe, including our own bodies. If you have ever been to an acupuncturist, you are familiar with the insertion of tiny sharp needles in specific areas to allow the qi to flow freely. It is thought that when the qi is permitted to flow without blockage, it then settles in the lower abdomen from whence it originates. This activates the parasympathetic nervous system, allowing healing to take place.

In Sanskrit, this same life force is called Prana. The word refers to the universal energy which flows through all living beings. It is the physical energy that enables our bodies to metabolize and move; it is the mental energy fueling our thoughts, emotions, and consciousness; it is our spiritual energy connecting us to the Divine.

Interestingly, the word Prana also refers to the breath, as if to say that breathing leads to more than just respiration, more than the mere exchange of oxygen and carbon dioxide at a molecular level. The breath is recognized as a gift, enhancing the flow of the life force within the body.

The practice of Pranayama or breathwork, is the conscious regulation of the breath. It enhances the flow of the breath (or the life force) within the body, and has been linked not only to improved lung capacity, endurance, and oxygenation of the tissues, but also to mental clarity and emotional regulation.

Exploring the Therapeutic Benefits of Pranayama (Yogic Breathing): A Systematic Review, published in 2020 in the *International Journal of Yoga*, found the practice of pranayama to improve breathing in patients with asthma, heighten immune function in cancer patients, lower blood pressure, improve anxiety, reduce depression, and foster better sleep.

Thank you for your patience. Hang in there.

Now let's take a closer look at the passage of Scripture mentioned at the start of this week's meditation. It describes an interaction of Jesus with his disciples following his resurrection. John 20:21 states that Jesus breathed on them, prior to invoking a blessing—*Receive the Holy Spirit.* Why the breath? Why not just impart the Holy Spirit? We are familiar with the laying on of hands when a blessing is provided, but breath?

The Greek word here for *breathed on* is ἐνεφύσησεν, or in English letters enephysesen, and it is found only in John 20:22, nowhere else in the New Testament. Where it is found however is in the ancient Greek translation of the Old Testament called the Septuagint. Here the word is found in Genesis 2:7.

Then the LORD God formed a man from the dust of the ground and (enephysesen) breathed into his nostrils the breath of life, and the man became a living being. -John 20:22, New International Version

It seems that the breath of God or of the resurrected Jesus had some power behind it ... the power, in fact, to impart life.

Are you still there?

A more commonly found word in the New Testament is the Greek word πνεῦμα or pneuma. It is translated as air in motion, breath, or wind.

But interestingly, this same pneuma is also translated as spirit or ghost, including the Holy Ghost or Spirit. I like to consider that when Jesus breathed on his disciples, he was imparting the Holy Spirit. For all intents and purposes, he *spirited on them.*

Pneuma ... the word for wind and for spirit. Same word for both! It's breath and it's life and it's Spirit. It's life-giving breath. It's life-giving spirit. It's a dancing wind. It's the dancing third person in the Holy Trinity. It's hard to see where one ends and the other begins.

Questions for Reflection:

1. Have you learned anything from this study in words, perhaps something that deepens your understanding of Scripture?
2. Is it new to you to consider Eastern concepts such as qi and Prana along with the Biblical concept of pneuma? How do you feel about this?
3. Do you think it is valid to consider the breath as a life force? What does this mean?
4. What do breath and wind and spirit have in common? How are they different? Do you think the English words convey different nuances than the catch all *pneuma*?
5. The Greek word *pneuma* is neutral; in other words, it has neither a masculine nor a feminine connotation. The word *ruach* on the other hand, which is the Hebrew word for breath, wind, and spirit is actually feminine. How does this deepen your understanding of the third person of the Trinity?

Contemplative Practice: Having laid a foundation, we are going to focus for the next few weeks on breathwork. Because maybe, just maybe when we draw breath into our lungs, in some way that our western minds find it difficult to grasp, we also draw in a life force, or maybe even something spiritual.

Let's increase the time we spend meditating to four minutes, shall we? We will begin as we always do, finding a comfortable place and drawing our attention to our surroundings, then to our bodies, and finally to our breath.

After approximately two minutes of noticing, we will begin to manipulate our breath with a practice known as belly breathing or abdominal breathing. (The timing of this is not really important, but you can set a timer for two minutes and then for one minute longer if you wish.

On each inhalation, we first fill our bellies, then we feel our rib cages expand, and finally we feel the rise of our collarbones. On the exhalation, we feel the collarbones drop, then we feel the rib cage relax, and finally the naval draws back toward the spine. Continue with your belly breathing until the end of your meditation time.

WEEK 5

READING: PSALM 36: 5-9

How precious is your lovingkindness, O God!
Therefore the children of men put their trust
under the shadow of your wings.
They are abundantly satisfied with the
fullness of your house,
And you give them drink from the river of your pleasures.
For with you is the fountain of life;
In your light we see light.

Psalm 36: 7-9, New King James Version

Have you ever had an artistic encounter that created what could best be described as a sense of longing? Perhaps even a feeling of homesickness?

I will never forget the first time I saw the film *The Lord of the Rings* at the movie theatre. While I think Tolkien captured that longing for adventure and the magic of Middle Earth in all of us, the most powerful image for me was Rivendell, the home of the elves.

In case you have missed out on the fantasy spun by JRR Tolkien, suffice it to say that a gentle and ordinary hobbit has an astounding and unlikely adventure, part of which involves being hosted by the elves in their exquisite and unspoiled land. It's like a rain forest without the snakes and spiders: rushing waterfalls, sparkling greenery, gorgeous blooms of flowers. If I could have packed up and moved to Rivendell the day I first saw the movie, I surely would have.

The thing is I felt like I belonged there, and by some mistake of magic I had been transposed to a small American suburb to live out my days. I had perhaps been switched at birth, unawares. (I have normal ears, by the way, and do not look anything like an elf.)

Now I am the last person with any fixed theological answers—certainly not those pertaining to other realms beyond the one in which we currently find ourselves. However, I know this: When I read this passage from Psalm 36, it reminds me of Rivendell, for which I remain homesick. And if I feel homesick, if I have a sense of yearning, the details of which evade my grasp, then maybe there is something tangible for which I long. I can only hope that it is something like Rivendell.

Frederick Buechner wrote extensively about the idea that all of us hunger for the Kingdom of God, as it exists in its purest sense. He believed that even though we are unable to identify or recognize it, the Kingdom is where we belong and we are homesick for it.

So how do we find that for which we are so homesick, that for which our hearts long? Is this Kingdom in another realm? Is it a place accessible after death to those who have lived faithfully? If the Kingdom of God is a place where God is king, and certainly that makes sense, it does not seem as if the world which we inhabit is that kingdom. So where is it, and how do we find it?

In Luke 17:20-21, the Pharisees, those renowned followers of Jewish law, ask Jesus when they might expect the coming of the Kingdom of God, and Jesus answers them with this:

The Kingdom of God does not come with observation; nor will they say, 'See here!' or 'See there!' For indeed, the Kingdom of God is within you.

Now here is the interesting thing about this verse. The word translated *within* can also be translated *among* or *in your midst*, and quite often it is, especially by theologians who cannot wrap their minds around the possibility that the Kingdom of God might possibly be found even in the most self-righteous of Pharisees. But the Greek word in question, *entos*, is found only in one other place in the Scriptures, again during an interaction with the Pharisees.

In Matthew 23:26, Jesus encourages these scholars whose life's work is the study of and adherence to the laws of Moses, to focus instead on their hearts rather than on outward appearances. *First clean the inside* (entos) *of the cup and dish*, says Jesus *and then the outside also will be clean.*

I like to think, therefore, that Jesus is actually saying that the Kingdom of God is within us. It's that close, that accessible. We need not feel homesick; we need only to notice.

This is the beauty of meditation, of mindfulness, of contemplative prayer: It's a means of turning our attention toward the treasure that is contained within us, that which has been there all along, but that perhaps in our distraction, we failed to notice. Let's commit to this practice, shall we, even if it is just for a few minutes a day? Let's spend just a few minutes drinking from the river of the pleasures of God, seeking the abundant satisfaction that is found in the Divine house (or Kingdom).

Questions for Reflection:

1. What is your favorite form of art? It is music? Film? Painting? Literature? Why?
2. Have you ever experienced a feeling of what you might describe as unexplained homesickness? What were the circumstances?
3. What are your thoughts regarding the ideas of Frederick Buechner? He states that we are *starving to death* for the Kingdom of God. Do you believe that possibility or is this statement too strong?
4. Do you think Jesus was telling the Pharisees that the kingdom was in their midst or within them? What is your reason?

5. What are the implications of the Kingdom of God being within us? How might it change you to view yourself and others as carrying such a treasure?
6. Reflect on your times of meditation thus far. Has it been easy or difficult for you? Are you seeing any value to such a practice?

Contemplative Practice: The name of God in the Hebrew bible is YHWH—the scholarly consensus being that it should be pronounced *Yahweh*. But other scholars and rabbis believe that the addition of the vowels is incorrect. I find the interesting thing about this word, this name of God, is that if the focus is more on the consonants, it sounds a little bit like an inhalation followed by an exhalation. Breathe in: *Yah*. Breathe out: *Weh*.

... sounds like a nice meditation option to me.

So begin as always in a comfortable spot, drawing your attention from the outside world into yourself. But this time, when you begin to focus on your breath, eventually moving on to belly breathing, try breathing in and out the Name of God. Inhale: *Yah*. Exhale: *Weh*.

WEEK 6

READING: JONAH 1

Now the word of the LORD came to Jonah, the son of Amittai, saying, 'Arise, go to Nineveh, that great city and cry out against it; for their wickedness has come up before Me.' But Jonah arose to flee to Tarshish from the presence of the LORD. He went down to Joppa and found a ship going to Tarshish; so he paid the fare, and went down into it, to go with them to Tarshish from the presence of the LORD.

Jonah 1: 1-3, New King James Version

Surely this cannot go well ...

Perhaps you are not familiar with the book of Jonah, the reluctant prophet. He was called to Nineveh, the notoriously cruel and violent capital of Assyria, to deliver a message. However, as we discover later in the story, Jonah really did not want the people of that city to turn from their ways; what he wanted was their destruction. So rather than heading north from Israel to Nineveh, he hopped on a boat and headed west toward Spain. A storm ensued. By the luck of the draw, it was determined that Jonah was the cause of the tempest. It seemed best to the ship's crew that Jonah be killed rather than everyone on board ending up at the bottom of the sea. Therefore, they pitched him overboard in a sacrificial attempt to quell the angry seas.

However, as we know, this was not the end of the line for the prophet. Allegedly, Jonah was swallowed by a fish.

Perhaps you read of the Chilean kayaker who found himself in the mouth of a humpback whale off the coast of Patagonia earlier this year. This young man was merely held in the mouth of the whale, kayak and all, before being spit out. His father captured it on video, which quickly went viral. The young man recounted the terror associated with thinking that he had been eaten. But this whale was smart enough not to swallow a small boat.

Not so, the large fish which was said to have swallowed Jonah. There he remained, the reluctant undigested prophet, for three days, at which point the fish *vomited Jonah onto dry land*, leaving him pretty much back where he started.

Imagine this prophet—wet, sandy, bedraggled, and covered in whatever else the fish had to eat—looking for all intents and purposes like something the cat dragged in. He was hungry, exhausted, dehydrated, and done fighting. If this is not a picture of humility ...

Have you been there, humiliated and exhausted with the effort of trying to do things your own way? *It's hard to kick against the goads.* (Acts 9:5) Maybe it's a job or a relationship that you are reluctant to leave. Maybe it's an addiction, or simply an unhealthy lifestyle choice.

When we find ourselves someplace we don't want to be as a result of our poor choices, we can either kick and scratch like a honey badger, or we can sit with it.

When we find ourselves in an unpleasant situation—somewhere dark and smelly and dangerous—we can try to fix, control, or rationalize it, or we can surrender to the process. Sometimes surrendering is all it takes, and we are spit out onto higher ground.

I apologize for throwing around phrases such as *surrender to the process*. I had to meditate on this phrase for a minute or two while I was watering my plants; I had to think about a clear way to convey what this means. What came to mind is the process of recovery outlined in what is known as *The Twelve Steps*. I am including the first three steps as described by the fellowship of Narcotics Anonymous.

1. *We admitted that we were powerless over our addiction, that our lives had become unmanageable.*
2. *We came to believe that a Power greater than ourselves could restore us to sanity.*
3. *We made a decision to turn our will and our lives over to the care of God as we understood Him.*

Often we are the last ones to see that our modus operandi is not effective, but to his credit, Jonah recognized that he had hit rock bottom and knew where to turn. So he cried out to God from the belly of the fish:

In my distress I called to the LORD, and he answered me. From deep in the realm of the dead I called for help, and you listened to my cry. -New International Version

It's probably a safe bet Jonah did not know that the plan was to be vomited onto dry land. He just turned his will and his life over to the care of his God.

It is worth mentioning that Jonah got a second chance. *Now the word of the Lord came to Jonah a second time.* (Jonah 3:1) Guess which direction he headed.

Questions for Reflection:

1. Jonah wanted no part in helping the Ninevites escape what he felt they deserved. How do you feel about that?
2. Can you think of a person or group of people that you honestly feel should get what they deserve? Perhaps someone who has been convicted of a heinous crime, or a group of people responsible for the systematic genocide of another group?
3. Can you remember a time when you were fighting to stay in a situation that you knew was not best for you? Are you there now? What is the draw?
4. What do you find difficult to surrender? What are you fighting to keep?
5. God very clearly asked something of Jonah, and he very

clearly refused. This did not go well for him. Have you ever had such an experience? Were you given a second chance?

Contemplative Practice: Today's practice is known as a loving-kindness meditation. We begin as always in a quiet and comfortable spot, and in a comfortable position. We notice our surroundings and then draw our attention inward, eventually just focusing on the breath. When you feel ready, choose a simple prayer for yourself, something along these lines:

May I be well.

May I be happy.

May I be at peace.

Then bring to mind someone you truly love, and who you believe loves you too. Extend those words to them as well.

May you be well.

May you be happy.

May you be at peace.

Next bring to mind someone you know (or know of) but are not particularly close with. You might not even have a relationship with this person. Extend the blessing to this person too:

May you be well.

May you be happy.

May you be at peace.

Now allow your mind to rest on someone toward whom you do not have particularly warm feelings. It could be a public figure. It could be someone who has caused you harm in some way. Bless them with your prayer.

May you be well.

May you be happy.

May you be at peace.

If you like, you can spend more time in each category, as there may be others toward whom you would like to extend your loving-kindness. Or you can just trust that the first person who came to mind in each category is the one who especially needs your kind and loving words. When you are ready, gently blink your eyes and open them. Your meditation is complete.

WEEK 7

READING: JOHN 15: 1-11

I am the vine, you are the branches. He who abides in me, and I in him, bears much fruit; for without me, you can do nothing.

John 15: 5, New King James Version

In 1955, Anne Morrow Lindbergh took a vacation. By herself. She left her husband and five children at home and took off for the beach. By herself for the first week, and joined by her sister for the second, she spent her days wandering by the sea, collecting shells in the morning and writing in the afternoon. When she chose a shell, she did so because of what it seemed to speak to her. The lessons of the seashells became the short classic work *Gift From the Sea.*

In the preface, Lindbergh states that the meditative musings contained within the book were her attempt to work things out for herself, to strike a balance between a multitude of obligations. Yet many people have benefited because she elected to share her meditations with the world at large.

Write a book, people have said to me. But honestly, writing has never come easily to me. It's always been a struggle to find the right words (even with suggestions from my friend AI Chat). I've tried, and among other roadblocks, I get so hung up on citing sources. Because, after all, no idea is truly mine, is it?

One morning I thought about the fact that for about fifty years, I have made it a daily practice to spend time in spiritual pursuits, seeking a relationship with the God of my understanding. This has taken a myriad of forms over the years—silent meditation, reading, study, journaling, praying out loud, music, you name it. *What if I were to simply share some of the experiences I have had, some reflections, some spiritual musings? Might that not serve as a guide to others on their spiritual journeys?*

Frankly, my friends, here is where the magic happened. When I stopped pretending to try to teach others, and instead just shared from my own personal experience, the words poured out of me. I felt like a conduit—some might say like a branch connected to the Vine.

But it's not just about the writing, you understand. That's only the metaphor. It's the trust, the surrender, the allowing of the energy of God to flow like sap, nourishing and sustaining the fragile branch.

There's no need for anxiety, because, as branches of the

Vine, we no longer need to fix or control things. We live mindfully and contemplatively, discerning guidance in all the events of our lives. Our chief work is to stay connected, because without the support of the Vine, we wither.

If we maintain the connection to the Divine Flow (and this may look different for you than it does for me), not only do we flourish but we *bear much fruit*. And this is what we all truly desire, isn't it? We want significance—we want our lives to have meaning; we want the world to be a better place because we spent some time here.

Now for you, the fruit may be obvious. Perhaps you can point to amazing work that you have been a part of. If so, I am very happy for you. Thank you for staying connected to the Vine and allowing God to work through you.

But for most of us who live a rather obscure existence, sojourning on in our little corner of the planet, we have to trust. We try not to mess up our children too badly. We try to limit our use of plastic. We do our best not to snap at people who irritate us. We do our best not to impede the Divine Flow which is supposed to be responsible for the fruit. We get out of the way ... again. You may be fortunate enough to see the fruit resulting from your connection to the Vine; you may not. But you know what? The promise is real. Just stay connected.

Questions for Reflection:

1. What does it mean to you to *stay connected* to God?
2. What has been your experience of surrender? Is this an easy or difficult process for you?
3. Let's review the first three steps of The Twelve Steps of Narcotics Anonymous quoted in last week's meditation:

   Step 1. We admitted that we were powerless over our addiction, that our lives had become unmanageable.

   Step 2. We came to believe that a Power greater than ourselves could restore us to sanity.

   Step 3. We made a decision to turn our will and our lives over to the care of God as we understood Him.

For some of us, it is only the unmanageability of our lives or simply a troublesome situation that convinces us to turn our will and our lives over to God. Can you relate to this?

4. What *fruit* have you seen in your own life which seems to be a direct result of your connection to the Vine? What would you like to see more of?
5. How do you feel about the idea that you may not be fortunate enough to see the fruit resulting from your connection to the Vine? Is there an area where you find yourself simply trusting that fruit will be produced?

Contemplative Practice: Light is often a metaphor for God as well as everything that is good, holy, gracious, and wise. It is symbolic of hope and divine revelation. That being said, today's meditation will involve a focus on light.

We begin as always with finding a comfortable and quiet spot, noticing our surroundings and then drawing our attention inward.

Once you feel ready, begin to notice a warm yellow light surrounding you. Feel yourself bathed in that light, noticing the warmth on your skin. Then, as you breathe in, actually inhale the light; feel it traveling into your lungs. As you exhale, imagine the light traveling all through your body. Feel it in your abdominal cavity, warming all your organs. Imagine the light traveling down through your arms and legs and into your fingers and toes. With each breath in, draw in more light, and with each breath out, feel it dispersing throughout your body. If there is any discomfort in your body, draw the light toward that area and allow it to bring healing. Be certain to allow the light into your brain to bring a sense of calm and an experience of joy. When you feel ready, gently blink your eyes open. Your meditation is complete.

Week 8

Reading: Galatians 5: 17-25

But the fruit of the Spirit is love, joy, peace, patience, kindness, goodness, faithfulness, gentleness and self-control. Against such things there is no law.

Galatians 5: 22-23, New American Standard

During Lent one year, I worked through Matthew Kelly's *Journal for the Last Quarter of Your Life* because now more than ever, in my golden years I wish to *live deliberately*. One of the challenges of that journal was to pick a spiritual gift—a fruit, if you will—on which to focus for the last quarter of my life. Now many of these gifts frankly seem like a lot of work. Patience, love, self-control ... I want these things, of course. Who doesn't? But it seems exhausting to focus on any of them. I admire those of you who are good at them. I really do.

But then I realized that I could focus on joy. What? If joy is a spiritual gift, a fruit, then could I really pick that one? Could I approach each day considering what would bring me joy? It seems like cheating, doesn't it?

But honestly, what if the world was filled with joyful people—people living their best life, embracing who they really are, choosing what is most meaningful? What if the world was filled with people who have abandoned the trivial, soul-sucking, superficial pursuit of materialism, one-upmanship, and entertainment?

Most people agree that there is a difference between happiness and joy. It's fun to be happy, and we all enjoy it. Certainly, there is nothing wrong with that; it's just kind of hard to maintain because it is so dependent on external factors. It's hard to feel happy when things are not going well. Joy, on the other hand, is deep and abiding, and less dependent on what is going on in the moment. In a New York Times article, David Brooks sums this up beautifully, explaining that happiness usually reflects our own values, whereas joy transcends our very self. Brooks goes on to describe joy as a gift received in the context of giving away oneself and one's own gifts. While he certainly does not disdain happiness, he believes that joy is far better. He advocates for enjoying happiness whenever we find it, but more importantly working to put ourselves in a position in which it is likely that we will receive joy. This is the greater gift.

It's easy to think of things that bring happiness—spending time with people we enjoy, a vacation, an enjoyable hobby, a good job, a good book, a good meal.... (Note that happiness is directly related to factors external to ourselves.) Joy, on the other hand, arises from within and is often related to a sense of purpose and meaning. It is possible to be happy and joyful, but it is also possible to be joyful, independent of happiness—to be joyful even though external circumstances may be less than desirable or even dire.

So I can wake up in the morning and ask myself how I can structure my days in order to bring myself happiness in the fourth quarter of my life, and there is nothing wrong with that. But I might be remiss if I did not ask myself how might I spend my time, what decisions might I make, what might I give up, what could I give away, with the end goal being an unshakeable, boundless, enduring joy which will see me through some of the fourth quarter challenges that may make me feel a little bit less than happy.

Questions for Reflection:

1. What makes you happy? What brings you joy? Do these answers feel different or similar?
2. Do you know someone who you might consider a joyful person? What do you think their secret may be?
3. Reflect on the ideas of David Brooks. What are your thoughts?
4. What does not bring you joy? Are there changes you can make to eliminate this from your life?
5. What changes do you feel called to make so that your life bubbles over with infectious joy, making you someone people truly love to be around?

Meditation: Spend several minutes in silence, allowing yourself to be filled with joy. With each inhalation, breathe in joy. With each exhalation, breathe out any thoughts, emotions, desires that might be impeding the joy you deserve to experience. Your practice might look something like this:

Breathe in joy. Breathe out worry.

Breathe in joy. Breathe out pain.

Breathe in joy. Breathe out selfishness.

Breathe in joy. Breathe out fear.

You get the idea.

Option: On other days this week, you might choose a different trait that you would like to see more of in your life. Maybe you would like to be more peaceful. If so, you could breathe in peace and breathe out those things that are stealing your peace.

Perhaps you would like to be more kind. If so, breathe in kindness and breathe out whatever stands in the way of the kind person you truly are.

Week 9

Reading: Luke 15: 11-32

'My son,' the father said, 'you are always with me and everything I have is yours. But we had to celebrate and be glad, because this brother of yours was dead and is alive again, he was lost and is found.'

Luke 15: 31-32, New International Version

Let me ask you a question: Who do you relate to in this story? If it is the younger son, then I am very happy for you. You understand grace and mercy in a very personal way; you are closer to the Kingdom of God than many of us.

I find that my sympathies lie with the older brother instead. Here is the view from where I sit: Rather than enjoying his father who clearly loves him very much, the younger brother has the audacity to say, *When you die, this money is going to be mine anyway. How about you just give it to me now because who knows how long you're going to live?*

For reasons that are unclear to me, the father hands over the money to his impetuous offspring. Having then secured the funds, the boy takes off for a distant country, (I picture him in Dubai.) and quickly runs through the money. It is unclear what the extent of his vices are, but there is a mention of prostitutes and *wild living*. The details are left to our imagination.

So it surprises no one when the money runs out. And when things look dire, the young man decides to head for home. The other option appears to be either starvation or the tending of swine. Now, working with hogs is a job to which no self-respecting Jewish man would lower himself, as the animal is unclean according to the laws of Moses. So our hero elects not to engage in this unclean work, prostitutes and wild living notwithstanding. I suppose you have to draw the line somewhere.

He rehearses his lines: *Father, I have sinned against heaven and against you. I am no longer worthy to be called your son, make me like one of your hired servants.* One pictures him muttering this to himself on the long journey home.

As the story goes, the father spotted his son *while he was still a long way off.* He took off running and met him in the distance, wrapping his arms around his youngest in a big bear hug. The son begins with his rehearsed speech: *Father, I have sinned* ... but he cannot even get the words out of his mouth before the party begins. A party with a slaughtered calf, music, and dancing.

Meanwhile, where is the older brother? The same place he has been since the beginning of the story: Devoted to his father, he is fulfilling responsibilities, working day in and out, doing everything asked of him, shouldering the additional work left to him by his absent sibling.

And apparently no one even bothered to come tell him that he could take the afternoon off to join the party. Did they forget about him or what? Picture him: sweaty, dusty, thirsty, hungry, weary, plodding in from the fields. As he draws closer, he begins to catch the strains of music, the clinking of glasses, and the smell of a barbecue. A servant had to apprise him of the day's events.

The older brother became angry and refused to go in.

Well, I say *Who can blame him?* I'm angry just writing about it. There is nothing fair or just about this. The younger brother got what he did not deserve, while it appears that the responsible, hardworking, devoted son was overlooked.

This does not sit well with us, does it? We are wired and programmed with a sense of fairness; we believe we are entitled to certain privileges based on our hard work and good ethical practices. It's the American way—the American dream, right?

Worse yet, this is a parable about God, those who have wandered away from him, and apparently those who have not wandered away.

But a good hard look at this philosophy reveals its fallacies. ... turns out it's not that simple, and those of us who think we got what we deserved because we pulled ourselves up by our bootstraps have probably been gifted with more than we realize. We are all recipients of grace. The rain falls on the just and the unjust.

The sullen pouting of the older brother kept him from joining the party. Instead of drinking and feasting and dancing, he remained outside, no doubt becoming increasingly angry—feeding his sense of entitlement while punishing himself.

Brothers and sisters, we have the same choice, don't we? We can insist on the exhausting process of keeping score, deciding who deserves what, or we can let go and join the Divine Dance of mercy, generosity, and blessing.

'My son,' the father said, 'You are always with me and everything I have is yours. But we had to celebrate and be glad, because this brother of yours was dead and is alive again; he was lost and is found.'

Questions for Reflection:

1. Who do you most relate to in the story of the prodigal son?
2. Can you think of a situation where you really felt that you wanted someone to get what they deserved? (Most of us can.) Do you feel justified in that opinion?
3. As parents (or grandparents), most of us strive hard to make certain that our children are treated equally, so no resentments arise. What are your thoughts about the

parenting choices of the father? (This may be a hard question to answer, as we are used to thinking of this father as symbolizing God. But if it makes you feel more comfortable evaluating the father, remember that in a parable, not every detail is necessarily symbolic. It is the overall lesson taught by the parable that is important.)

4. Gautama Buddha is quoted as saying that *anger is punishment we give ourselves for someone else's mistake.* What are your thoughts regarding this quote as it relates to the parable?
5. Most people believe they have worked hard for what they have, be it material possessions, good relationships, robust health, or merely an optimistic outlook on life. Certainly it is possible to find Scripture to support this view, and many proponents of the prosperity gospel have done so. What do you believe?

Contemplative Practice: This week we will practice another loving-kindness meditation.

Begin in your usual manner, emptying your mind of anxious thoughts and focusing each of your senses on your surroundings. Draw your attention inward, focusing on your own body. Take a few belly breaths. Then just let your mind wander. See if someone pops into your mind; if so, take a moment to offer blessings to them. Feel free to use the blessing that you chose for the last loving-kindness meditation, or choose a new one— whatever seems appropriate to you. After you have blessed that person, let them depart.

Wait quietly for the next person to come to mind, and extend your blessing to them as well. Continue this process with each person who appears in your conscious mind, blessing them and subsequently dismissing them. After a time, you may notice that people start to line up, each waiting for their turn. Bless each of them.

When there is a lull in the activity, draw your attention back to yourself. Take one more deep breath. Your meditation is complete.

Week 10

Reading: Matthew 13: 24-29

Let the weeds and the wheat grow together until the harvest time.

Matthew 13:30, New Century Version

Have you had the assistance of a toddler in your garden? Maybe you advised the child that if he or she helped with some weeding, then an opportunity to use the garden hose might present itself. (Everyone knows there is no joy like that of playing with a garden hose—including the possible joy of spraying the dog or a sibling.)

So you crouch down together. You patiently point out the delicately sprouting vegetables, congratulating yourself on teaching important lessons about where food comes from, as well as actually accomplishing something. *And these are weeds,* you say, pointing them out. *We pull these out so our vegetables will grow big and strong.* Of course, while things may start out well, it is not long before your precious vegetables have been violently torn from their carefully cultivated bed. This is the danger of weeding with a young child.

While you are pulling the weeds, you may uproot the wheat with them. Let both grow together until the harvest.

Now I think it is safe to say that most of us consider ourselves to be wheat and others weeds. Be honest. I bet you can think of a few weeds who are really a problem, some that are impeding your blossoming and growth, crowding out your sunshine, and generally robbing you of what you need to thrive. And that's okay. You're probably right.

But it's a question of surrender. The weeds are there and will remain there, apparently for quite some time. Our life project is to learn to love the weeds sown among us. We don't have to accept bad behavior, but we are called to love.

I see you, weed. I see your faults. I care for you anyway. I will let you grow. I might even share something with you that will help you thrive.

Because what happens when we start yanking out the weeds in our lives? We damage the wheat. We damage ourselves and others in the process.

And let's be honest, no one of us is entirely weed or entirely wheat anyway, are we? When we target any one person, no matter how much of a weed they seem to be, we risk collateral damage. It seems to me a better solution would be the cultivation of our own souls, calling out the wheat within us, strengthening it, feeding and watering it. If the wheat is strong enough, the weeds are no threat.

Questions for Reflection:

1. What or who are the weeds in your life? What crowds your sunshine and robs you of what you feel you need to thrive?
2. What has been your experience in uprooting the weeds around you? Have you been successful?
3. Can you think of some weeds that, while problematic, may simply need to remain? What will be your response to them?
4. Have you had an experience which has been damaging to you when you were trying to uproot weeds?
5. What will you do this week to cultivate your own soul?

Meditation: Can you spend five minutes in a guided meditation? ... bet you can.

After you get comfortable, notice your surroundings, then draw your attention inward. Begin to imagine yourself standing before a stone wall covered with vines. Looking closely, you see an old wooden door with an antique handle. You open the door and find yourself in the most amazing secret garden. The sun is rising and the garden is wet with dew. There is a gentle breeze moving.

You spend some time wandering through this garden of your mind, taking time to focus on each plant you pass. Notice the colors and the way the sun plays upon the leaves, the blossoms, and the fruit. The dew sparkles.

When you reach the other side of the garden, you find a bench. You sit quietly on the bench, the sun warm on your face, the gentle breeze moving. You close your eyes and focus on the experience: You breathe in the aroma of the blooming flowers. You listen to the song of the birds. You feel perfectly serene, knowing there is nowhere else you need to be at this moment. You are filled with gratitude.

When you feel ready, rise from the bench and walk slowly out of the garden. Gently blink your eyes open. Your meditation is complete.

Week 11

Reading: Matthew 25: 31-46

I was in prison, and you came to me.

Matthew 25:36, New King James Version

Toward the end of the twentieth century, there was a movement to deinstitutionalize the mentally ill. With the advent of the first antipsychotic medication, Thorazine, and others that followed it, many patients who previously had been institutionalized for their own safety and the safety of others were able to be stabilized. Long stays in psychiatric hospitals were replaced with routine outpatient therapy provided in the context of community mental health services.

Although this has been a positive change for many people, the policy left some extremely vulnerable people without care, largely because the very nature of severe mental illness often presents with disorganization, paranoia, and a lack of resources, making it very difficult for such patients to seek and successfully obtain treatment in the community.

The delusions which can accompany illnesses such as schizophrenia and bipolar disorder may on very rare occasions lead those suffering with these disorders to commit crimes. Tragically some of them are violent in nature. Hence, such unfortunate men and women end up incarcerated. What to do then?

One solution is to try to create a sort of psychiatric hospital within the walls of the prison.

I share all this to say that I once worked within the prison system, providing mental health services to severely ill incarcerated men and women. In fact, I worked on a tier that was set aside for individuals who were in crisis, and I treated the most unstable of these inmates. It was a great experience, and I would like to share with you one of the most powerful lessons I learned while working behind the walls of a maximum security prison:

In prison there are well established churches, all run by inmates. Each church has a pastor, as well as an assistant—one who can step into the pastor's shoes in case something should happen to the leader. And let me tell you, these men and women know their stuff. With no shortage of time (many of them in for life), they study and study Scripture, commentaries, and books of theology. Unfettered by a lot of the obligations that serve to distract us, dwelling in cells reminiscent of those occupied by nuns, monks, and anchorites, they are men and women of prayer and devotion.

One day at the prison I found myself speaking with the prison chaplain, a civilian hired by the state to serve the religious needs of the inmates. He said to me, *What am I supposed to do with all of these church people who want to come in and volunteer?* He went on to say that there seems to be a mistaken idea that these poor, lonely, and desperate prisoners need the good news of Jesus. Who better to do that than suburban church members, possibly of a different race and socioeconomic stratum? (Pardon the sarcasm.)

So what is the reason church groups are lining up to come into prisons, and what is it they think that they will find there? I can only assume that it has something to do with the passage of Scripture mentioned at the beginning of this meditation. Jesus had some pretty clear criteria for separating the sheep from the goats, and the temptation for all of us is to check a box:

> Feed someone? Easy. Sign up to serve a meal at a homeless shelter during the holidays. But you better sign up a few months in advance.
>
> Give someone a drink? You bet. A quick Google search will direct you to organizations like water.org where you can click the donate button.
>
> Taking care of someone who is sick? ... pretty sure we've all done that at some point.
>
> Providing clothing to someone who needs it? *Honey, can you please drop this bag off at the thrift store?*
>
> Welcome a stranger? A little bit less comfortable, but there are multiple organizations working with refugees if your political persuasion allows for this.
>
> Visit Jesus in prison? On it.

Certainly I cannot judge another's motives. But what I do know is that the church behind the wall has a lot to teach *us*.

What if the visit to prison is just an opportunity to connect with incarcerated brothers and sisters, to just be together and maybe to be humble enough to realize that those of us on the outside may be the beneficiaries? It is Jesus we're visiting after all.

Questions for Reflection:

1. What has been your experience with the penal system? Perhaps you or someone you know has been incarcerated. Perhaps you or someone you know has been the victim of a violent crime and the perpetrator is incarcerated.
2. What kind of thoughts or emotions come to mind when you think of prisons or jails or the people who reside behind their walls?

3. What is your reaction to the information provided regarding the church within the prisons?
4. Do you have any experience with groups of people who are providing resources for incarcerated men and women? How effective have these groups or organizations been?
5. What does it mean to you that Jesus would associate himself so closely with individuals who are incarcerated, *actually saying I was in prison and you visited me?*

Contemplative Practice: *We do not know what to pray for as we should, but the Spirit herself intercedes for us with groanings too deep for words; and God who searches the hearts knows what the mind of the Spirit is, because she intercedes for the saints according to the will of God.* -Romans 8:26-27

If this is the case, then what is our job when it comes to prayer? Maybe it's simply to get out of the way while the God within us communicates with the God beyond us. In 1975, a group of three Trappist monks who studied the 14th Century classic *The Cloud of Unknowing* proposed a means of communing with God which lies beyond conversation. They referred to the practice as centering prayer. I am providing you with the brothers' four steps to centering prayer for this week's suggested contemplative practice:

1. Begin as you have become accustomed, sitting comfortably with your eyes closed. Scan your body for any held tension, and make a conscious effort to relax.
2. Choose a sacred word which indicates to you that you fully intend to place yourself in the presence of God, and that you are surrendered to any divine activity within you.
3. Continue to sit quietly, allowing your sacred word to symbolize for you divine presence and divine action.
4. Should any distracting thought, emotion, perception or image come to mind, simply return to your sacred word. It serves as your anchor.

WEEK 12

READING: ISAIAH 2: 2-5

They shall beat their swords into plowshares,
And their spears into pruning hooks;
Nation shall not lift up sword against nation,
Neither shall they learn war anymore.

Isaiah 2: 4, New King James Version

I find this verse to be a stunning example of some of the beautiful poetry the Bible offers. So captivated have I been by this verse that in the seventies I wore a *plowshare.* It was a small pin, allegedly forged from a piece of some sort of weapon. The weapon was probably not a sword, but perhaps something even more ugly and violent.

In case this passage is new to you, allow me to speak for a moment about old-fashioned implements of farming:

In order to ready a field for planting, the earth must be prepared. One method of doing so prior to the industrial age involved pushing a plow through the soil to break up the earth. The plow contained one or more spikes as part of a coulter; its job was to break up the hard dirt. Then a piece called a moldboard would turn this soil over. The leading edge of the moldboard was known as the plowshare. Presumably the thinking is that the edge of a sword might be repurposed in the absence of war.

A pruning hook resembles a pole saw. There is a long pole, the end of which contains a curved saw blade or sickle. It can be used to trim vines or branches, especially when they are difficult to reach.

So the gist of this passage is the idea that there will come such a time of peace that weapons are rendered useless. One can imagine government officials wondering what to do with all these swords and spears, while the warriors are sitting around and getting fat.

When so much of a nation's resources have been spent on violent conquests and skirmishes, what is a nation to do? Perhaps one government official picked up a sword and thought *You know what this sharp edge reminds me of?*

So I wore my little plowshare as a kind of statement. That's how we made statements back then; we wore t-shirts and buttons, and put bumper stickers on our cars. The more committed of us had the option of marching and waving signs. I would venture to say this is pretty comparable to sharing a post on social media or changing your background photo. It makes you feel like you've done something without having to leave your couch. And if people like what you have posted, this increases the sense that you are making a difference. If you're lucky, maybe you can engage in a few social media arguments with people who hold differing opinions or political views.

But the work of shalom (the Hebrew word for peace) is hard work. This word, which is also a common Jewish greeting, is not limited to the absence of strife or a feeling of calm; It denotes tranquility, prosperity, security, and completeness—circumstances without blemish. While we might say that our day on the river was peaceful, or that Queen Elizabeth reigned during both war and peacetime, we are not speaking of shalom.

There are many reasons why individuals or communities are not experiencing shalom, and we don't have to look very far to find them. It can be uncomfortable to consider the unequal distribution of resources in our world, and often we make ourselves feel better by trying to believe that we make our own beds, by feeling that people get what they deserve. If we want to help, some of us may put up controversial social media posts; that is certainly an option, similar to me wearing my plowshare pin. In fact, that might inspire someone who sees what we have done to take further steps themselves. But if we really want to be peacemakers (and I think we probably do), this might involve more effort. As one of those bumper stickers relayed, *If you want peace, work for justice.*

In 1986, Mark Gornik and Allen Tibbels were living comfortable lives in Maryland. What made them uncomfortable, however, was the knowledge that in a neighborhood very close to them, others were not having the same experience. Repenting for the corporate sins of an oppressive society, they moved into the very poor neighborhood of Sandtown Winchester, on the west side of Baltimore, with the idea that the needs of that community would become their needs as well. Gornik's book *To Live in Peace: Biblical Faith and the Changing Inner City* recounts their experiences, while providing inspiration for churches wanting to bring shalom to other struggling communities.

Following their move, they found wonderful welcoming people there who had been seeking shalom for the families of Sandtown for many years. But what Gornik and Tibbels brought to the table were knowledge, connections, and resources. Within two years, the new residents, working in partnership with those who were born and raised there, formed a church. Subsequently a school was built, a health center came in, and a job training and placement service was established to provide employment for area residents. Habitat for Humanity arrived, resulting in the rehabilitation of 300 homes. This is shalom.

If Gornik and Tibbels had not moved into the neighborhood, they would not have felt the needs so acutely. They came to understand firsthand what it is like to send your children to failing inner city schools wrought with violence. They sought good healthcare for their families. In cities like Baltimore with a powerful industrial past where blue collar jobs were once plentiful, far too many people have turned to selling drugs as a means of income. The residents of Sandtown (new and old) wanted their young neighbors to be trained and hired to engage in meaningful work. They wanted the empty houses around them to be renovated, not only so their neighbors could have safe and affordable housing, but because empty houses are havens for unscrupulous activity and nesting spaces for rats.

The prophet Jeremiah told the Babylonian captives who were living in a city far from the one they loved:

Seek the shalom of the city where I have caused you to be carried away captive, and pray to the LORD for it; for in its shalom, you shall have shalom.

Questions for Reflection:

1. Where do I see people who lack shalom in my circle of influence?
2. What talents or special abilities do I have that I could offer, with the goal of increasing the shalom either in the life of an individual or in my community?
3. What is the place of social media in affecting change?
4. Are you currently in a place of shalom? If not, is there anything you can do to change your current circumstance? Is there anyone you can ask for help?
5. The prophet Jeremiah says that in the shalom of the city (you are not particularly attached to) you shall have shalom. Can you think of ways that the shalom of your city might be beneficial to your family? What can you do to make that happen?

Contemplative Practice: Now that you are so good at meditating, we are going to take this on the road by practicing a walking meditation. The idea is to take the meditative process on a walk. This may be more difficult than it sounds as we are used to walking on autopilot, usually thinking of a thousand different things, most of them related to what we are going to do when we arrive at our destination. But you will be walking mindfully, paying attention to the placement of each foot and the sensations you feel. You will be noticing the temperature, the sounds, and the smells in the air around you. Perhaps you will be walking with no destination in mind, noticing your surroundings. You can pay attention to your breath if you like, or use the word from your contemplative prayer in order to disengage from your thoughts. You could practice a loving-kindness meditation, sending blessings either to people you encounter or to those who dwell in the homes you pass. There are many options. If you prefer, you may simply walk around your house in a meditative manner. Choose your adventure.

Conclusion

From 1942 to 1945, 100,000 Jewish men, women, and children passed through the Westerbork transit camp, located in the Dutch countryside. Most of these unfortunate individuals were on their way to being exterminated in the camps to the east. Only 5,000 Jews who passed through Westerbork during those years survived.

In 1943, a 29-year-old Jewish woman named Esther *Etty* Hillesum arrived at Westerbork with her family. She was on her way to Auschwitz. Prior to her departure for the transit camp, she gave her diaries to a friend with instructions that they be published should she not survive. The diaries, letters she wrote to friends from the transit camp, and a postcard she threw from a train were published in eighteen different languages as *Etty Hillesum, An Interrupted Life.*

The work is valuable, not merely for the firsthand descriptions of the horrors of the camps, but also for the spiritual awakening which Hillesum seems to have experienced in the midst of unimaginable suffering. She writes of hope, of beauty, of gratitude for her experience of God, and for perceived richness of the camp. She bears witness to the power of love, exhorting us to hold fast to the "little piece of God" in us, for the sake of the world in which we live.

This has been the purpose of these exercises—to find the God within us, to uncover the light, that it may blaze brightly.

I am grateful to you for sharing this journey with me. I am very hopeful that it has broadened your mind in some way, and perhaps even deepened your faith. I wish for you a stronger contemplative practice, leading you to begin to understand ... *how wide and how long and how high and how deep the love of Christ actually is, and to be filled up to the very brim of your being with the fullness of God.* (Ephesians 3:18-19) I honor the light of Christ that you carry within. Namaste.

ACKNOWLEDGEMENTS

How can I possibly list everyone who has played a role in this spiritual adventure of mine, the one that I wish to share with you? Honestly, if I have encountered you, I am probably indebted to you for some aspect of my spiritual development. Maybe you will recognize yourself in the pages of this book. I hope so. I am very thankful to each of you and for your contribution. As Ram Dass said, "We are all just walking each other home." It hasn't always been fun, as is the case with most adventures, but it truly has been a joy to walk with you.

That being said, I do wish to thank those who were kind enough to read this book, and to offer supportive comments and constructive criticism. Thank you, Stephen Kaiss, Bonney Daves and Keri Faircloth.

A special thank you to my fabulous editor, Mary Lib Morgan at Perfectly Penned. You were a pleasure to work with.

Thank you also to Stephanie Fowler, Andrew Heller, and Patty Gregorio at Salt Water Media.

NOTES

Dedication

Rumi, J. (1997). *The Essential Rumi* (D. Barkw, J. Moyne, A.J. Arberry, & R. Nicholson, Trans.). Castle Books.

Frontispiece

Browning, Elizabeth Barrett. (1864). *Aurora Leigh, Book Severn.* J. Miller.

Introduction

Frost, R. (1916) The road not taken. In *Mountain interval* (pp. 9-10). Henry Holt and Company.

Week 2

Dickinson, E. & Roberts Brothers, P., Todd, M.L., ed. (1894) *Letters of Emily Dickinson.* Boston: Roberts Brothers.

Oliver, Mary. (1990). *House of Light.* Beacon Press.

Week 3

King, M. L. (1963). *Letter From a Birmingham Jail.* Harper Collins.

Week 4

Jayawardena, R., Ranasinghe, P., Ranawaka, H., Gamage, N., Dissanayake, D., Misra, A (2020). *Exploring the Therapeutic Benefits of Pranayama (Yogic Breathing): A Systematic Review.* International Journal of Yoga 13(2), 99-110. https://pmc.ncbi.nlm.nih.gov/articles/PMC7336946/

Week 5

Buechner, F. (1992). *The Clown in the Belfry.* Harper and Row.

Week 6

Narcotics Anonymous World Services, Inc. (2008). *Narcotics Anonymous.* Hazelden Publishing.

Week 7

Lindbergh, A. (1983). *Gift From the Sea.* Pantheon Books.

Week 8

Hunt, A. & Kelly, M. (2022). *The Fourth Quarter of Your Life.* Wellspring.

Brooks, D. (2019 May 7). “The Difference Between Happiness and Joy.” *New York Times,* New York Edition. P 23. nytimes.com/2019/05/07/opinion/happiness-joy-emotion.html

Week 12

Gornik, M. (2002). *To Live in Peace: Biblical Faith and the Changing Inner City.* Wm B Eerdmans Publishing Co.

Conclusion

Hillesum, E. (1983). *An Interrupted Life: The Diaries, 1941-1943; and Letters from Westerbork.* Pantheon Books

Acknowledgements

Dass, Ram. (2018). *Walking Each Other Home: Conversations on Loving and Dying.* Sounds True.

www.ingramcontent.com/pod-product-compliance
Lightning Source LLC
LaVergne TN
LVHW072329100826
845147LV00005B/664